Robin Williams

A Biography of Robin Williams

Ziggy Watson

Table of Contents

Introduction

Anyone who has had more than a passing interest in comedy or acting has, at one point or another, been blown away by the genius of Robin Williams. It feels strange to call what he did "genius", but this biography would be very far from the first. The truth is, anyone that worked with him came away with the same feeling— "this guy is different."

And so, he was. His life was a charmed one, starting as a standup entertainer on the mean streets of San Francisco in the 70's, to becoming one of the world's premier actors and starring in award-winning films. Even the way in which he got his big break was atypical, taking a bit role in a failing TV show and creating a brand and a future for himself nearly overnight.

But, the root of all his genius and fame is his standup career. Williams was a master of the stage and had crowds reeling in delight for decades after he started. His frenetically paced monologues were completely unique and thoroughly entertaining. Williams could switch from character to character with startling ease and always seemed to be one step ahead of the audience's expectations.

Still, it is completely impossible to copy him. That's likely the most impressive aspect of Williams' style. There were so many that rushed to copy his pace, his impressions, his look—but none of them could ever create a convincing facsimile. It's something that audiences and fans could feel, more so than a brand of comedy or a school of acting. Everything Williams did was convincing, even when he was being sardonic and sarcastic, as he often would.

It seems unthinkable for any American to have grown up or lived in the period from 1980-2010, without being affected by a performance from Robin Williams. There wasn't a kid alive that didn't love *Mrs. Doubtfire* when they saw it. For many, that was their first taste of his comedy. That role is a great example of the type of performance the world came to expect from him.

It starts out with a petty, sad version of Williams that, although still funny, can feel his life falling apart. He decides to dress up as his children's nanny to spend time with them. It's a ridiculous premise that could only be driven by Williams' ability to evoke emotion at any point — even when dressed like an old woman. There are few, if any, that could have carried that film in the way that he did.

As it turned out, his life was much darker than we though, not unlike the titular character of Mrs. Doubtfire. Williams struggled with substance abuse for his entire adult life, with many victories and setbacks along the way. His health was always in question and eventually it all caught up to him. When he was 63, he killed himself by hanging.

The world reeled from the thought of one its most powerful funny men succumbing to depression and death the way that he did. It appalls that someone with such a bright outward appearance and profession could come to end their life in such a grisly way. There are few celebrity deaths that came as a bigger surprise.

For many who had grown up with his comedy and enjoyed his fatherly descent into more mainstream films, this was devastating. The outpour of support that came for his family can only be rivaled by the biggest pop stars. That is because Williams was much more than a celebrity. He was an old friend that you were excited to bring into your home, someone who you invited into your life knowing he'd have something to say to make it better.

There is, perhaps, no greater example of this than his relationship with Koko the Gorilla and Christopher Reeves. With Koko, zookeepers brought Williams in to see if she responded to his comedy in the same way that humans did. They got off famously and many incredible videos are passed around on the internet showing their heart-wrenching encounters. When news of his death reached her, even Koko was saddened.

Christopher Reeve on the other hand was a great friend of Robin's. They met at Juilliard as students and kept in contact for many years after as they both came into their own as celebrities. When Reeve was grievously injured in a horsing accident and subsequently paralyzed, his friend came by to visit him in the hospital.

From Reeve's own words, "He was the first one to show up down in Virginia when I was really in trouble. He came here one afternoon and just— thank God I wear a seatbelt in this chair because I would have fallen out laughing," Reeve continued. "It's funny. In the middle of a tragedy like this, in the middle of a depression, you can still experience genuine joy and laughter and love."

Inspiring that kind of reaction from someone who had just lost so much is a power that many cannot even fathom. Yet, with Williams, he possessed it like it was his own breath. There was nothing false or mean about his spirit, he just made people laugh. In a world that has so much to cry about, there may be no greater gift. In Williams, that gift could be shared with every man, woman, and child on Earth.

Affluent in the North

He was born Robin McLaurin Williams on July 21st, 1951 in Chicago, Illinois. Williams never had to worry much about making ends meet as a child. His father was a top-ranking executive for Ford Motor Company and would be away often for business. Leaving time and money for his wife and three sons to do with what they will. This would be the defining aspect of Williams' life, he never wanted for much, but he would find out that there are different struggles when you have all that you need.

His mother, Laurie McLaurin, was a former model from the deep south. He would often struggle to gain her attention and he once stated his belief that his struggle to entertain her is what bore the comedy within him.

Williams was a good Episcopal boy, even though his mother believed in Christian Science — a religion that believes it is a weakness to try to make yourself better when you are sick. It is a wonder if this aspect of his life had some part in his eventual and early death.

Williams would live in a small house in the North Shore area of the Chicago metropolis. He recalls, "We weren't living in a mansion. It was just a really nice little house in Lake Forest, but it was really lovely. I remember that being really good times for me." His relationship with Chicago would be an important part of his life, although he made his break in San Francisco and died in his Tiburon, California home. His last role was a TV series about a Chicago-based ad agency and he often made appearances at the legendary Chicago comedy troupe, Second City.

Williams had a normal life in Chicago and then his family was uprooted to move to Michigan. His father, closely tied to Ford Motors, would need the proximity to Detroit. So, Williams had to enter school as an unknown quantity, never a recipe for success in the halls of prepubescent learning. Throughout his education, he was bullied and mocked by many for his eccentricities. However, like most eventual stars, there was always that nugget of popularity and attraction. To that effect, he was also a great athlete and was involved in extracurriculars, including being elected as the head of the student body.

Perhaps as a nod to his future, Williams did struggle with being extroverted enough to make friends. He was an introverted child—more content to imagine alone in his room than to go outside and interact with his peers. It is often said that this can be a sign of intelligence (as well as mental problems) and it certainly seems that way for Williams. It's hard to imagine someone being so good at comedy but who also rarely chooses to interact with those that find him so humorous, but that was his lot in life.

It's possible his relationship with his father had a role to play in his withholding personality. Robert Williams was the son of a wealthy business owner, himself, but the family business went bankrupt before Robert came of age. This curdled the man, as his life then became defined by hardship and diversity. When it came time to give love to his obviously gifted son, he was often found lacking.

Laurie was much, much younger than his father. They represented something much closer to a "trophy" marriage than a traditional one, but this author will not presuppose the feelings of the deceased. She, clearly, had a lot more life to live and was often out and about, as well, either furthering her modeling career or engaging in other business.

Williams was often left alone in his giant house, a 40-room mansion in the Michigan countryside, free to think and feel what he wanted. Often, when people of such interesting personality are created, it is because they were forced to grow alone, free from the outside influences of the world that would have had him grow into the same type as his father. Instead, he created a whole separate world to live in and he was the sole master.

His mother, Laurie, would recall, "He put his toy soldiers—he had thousands of them—in those rooms, carefully divided according to period." Many children would hear stories like that and think that life could get no better. But with the isolation young Robin felt, came much darker problems over the years.

Williams would later recall creating friends in his mind to satisfy the need for the real-life accompaniment he was sorely lacking. In reality, from the moment he started school, he had trouble fitting in. If he wasn't ostracized because he was rich, he was bullied for being small. Without any reliable source of strength at home, Williams was, again, left to his own devices.

Much like his ability to entertain himself, however, he was intelligent enough to craft his odd image into something that everybody loves: humor. His story is not unique in this way. The Comedy Hall of Fame is filled with individuals who were forced to create comedy as a source of power when the world took every other avenue away from them. Today's nerds, geeks, weirdos, and outcasts become tomorrow's entertainers and personalities.

Still, for all his effort, he could never really cement himself as a figure in school because his family moved around constantly. As the son of an auto-industry executive, it wasn't uncommon for him to move once every few years. By the time high school came around for Robin, he needed to plant his feet and become something.

When Williams turned 16, his father suddenly had a change of heart. Not content with just owning a large house and a trophy wife, the elder Williams decided to set out to see more of the world. He moved his family to Tiburon, California, where Williams would spend his last moments. Robin took immediately to the San Francisco vibe. He began to dress in colorful garb that would seem more familiar to his present-day image.

Robin immediately took to the culture of San Francisco that was exploding with vibrant color at the time. It was the exact moment

the hippie movement began in Haight-
Asbury corner in the very city the young
man had recently moved. Everything about
it appealed to him — especially the
substances.

From the pages of the Atlantic:

*"The hippie 'scene' on Haight Street in San
Francisco was so very visual that photographers
came from everywhere to shoot it, reporters came
from everywhere to write it up with speed, and
opportunists came from everywhere to exploit its
drug addiction, its sexual possibility, and its
political or social ferment. Prospective hippies
came from everywhere for one "summer of love"
or maybe longer, some older folk to indulge their
latent hippie tendencies, and the police to contain,
survey, or arrest.*

"Haight" – old Quaker name – rhymed with "hate," but hippies held that the theme of the street was love, and the best of hippies like the best of visitors and the best of the police, hoped to reclaim and distill the best promise of a movement which might yet invigorate American movement everywhere."

It was at this time that he began to change from the quiet, shy little boy that he had been to the ridiculous, erratic man he would be from that point on. His behavior changed, his ideas changed, and the material that he would produce as an adult changed forever. Here was a place that a person could say or do most anything without being judged and he would always take that to heart.

Then, like a shot ringing out at night, it came to him. He would join the drama department and put all that imagination and effort into something that could entertain people. It was a smash success in his life and kept him busy for the next few years as he developed into a young man.

Growing up affluent certainly has its advantages. Williams was encouraged by his excellent teachers to pursue his talents in acting and he began to yearn for the next step. Williams always knew he was different and he seemed to succeed in every area he put his mind to. He was even a productive member of the school's wrestling team.

When he graduated at the top of his class, Williams could choose from whatever schools he wanted. His family was behind him and his grades were stellar. It may surprise you, then, that he did not immediately set off to become the Robin Williams that we all know and love. No, he decided to go to school for Political Science in order to become a diplomat.

Maybe in some alternate dimension, there is a version of Robin Williams that put together peace treaties instead of performances. In this reality, however, it was a doomed idea. Williams began his career as a diplomat at the Claremont Men's College. He studied there for some time to further his "career".

But Williams noticed something about himself in those days. There never seemed to be enough time to balance his serious studies with what was becoming a serious infatuation with the community theater. He began to take classes there and, slowly but surely, his life priorities reset themselves back to performing.

Williams could go on no longer as a shell of his potential. He decided to quit that school and go to a community college for the purposes of studying acting. It was a low-impact decision that gave him some time to hone his craft and didn't drive him to bankruptcy in the meantime. He excelled there, as you might expect from the future star, and completed a few productions of note along the way.

He was particularly notable for his portrayal of Fagin in the stage production of *Oliver*. Williams' role required him to be the smarmy ringleader of a group of thieving children. He taught them how to live on the streets and the kids would bring back a bounty for him regularly. Williams' brand of energetic insanity brought the role to life and gave cause for his drama teacher to believe that he could become something special.

But, this would not be the last school nor the last elder influence on the young Robin Williams. He was about to enter a program that would change his life forever. He would go from a nobody at a community college to one of the nation's most prized prospects in a matter of months. Williams was determined to make it and he knew the next step was none other than the internationally acclaimed school of the arts, Juilliard.

Juilliard Trained Actor

As you might have guessed, the looming specter of Williams' father was ever-present during these soul-searching years. The hardened son of a failed businessman never had any impractical dreams, he simply wanted to survive. It is a credit to him, then, that he gave his son the encouragement he needed to attend school for acting—on one condition. Robert Williams wanted his son Robin to study something practical on the side, just in case he was not the actor he thought he was.

So, Williams, ever the good son, enrolled in a welding class. It's uncertain if Williams would have followed through with welding if his creative career went bust, but it is certain that he attended his first class—and not many more. Williams was struck by the brazen warning the instructor gave, warning his students about the danger of going blind in the profession. Williams was understandably excited to learn, then, that he received a full ride to Juilliard, effective immediately.

With welding left behind, along with the hope of a simple, normal life, Williams went on to the New York institution that specializes in the performance arts. This was the chance of a lifetime, even then, not many lifetimes include this chance. Juilliard accepts only 20 of those kinds of students when they send out their scholarships — total. Williams was even given advanced billing, along with his eventual good friend Christopher Reeve, and started at an advanced level.

Said Reeve, "Robin and I came in at the third-year level, we were put in special advanced sections; often, we were the only students in a class. John Houseman had an idea of what the Juilliard actor should be—well spoken but a bit homogenized—so it's not surprising the teachers were thrown by Robin. He did a monologue of *Beyond the Fringe* that made us laugh so hard we were in physical pain; they said it was a 'comedy bit' not acting."

That was where the struggles at Juilliard began and ended for Williams and his strange new style. He had every tool he needed and the talent to boot, but the system he was a part of had no room for the kind of person he was. He was zany, off-the-wall, and colorful. They wanted stoic, calm, and heroic. That didn't stop Robin, however, he went on doing exactly what he was always going to do, regardless of how is teachers felt about him. For one, Juilliard was an excellent place to make connections, and Williams made plenty of them.

Chief among them was his Mr. Reeve, who was much closer to the style that Juilliard was used to. Reeve had a strong jaw and an unassuming acting style that had him bound for roles as a leading man. This was the type of student they needed.

Williams did have some success at Juilliard, however. He baffled one of the world's leading speech teachers in Edith Skinner by being able to reproduce drastically different dialects on the fly. His primary acting teacher would lament that his performances were nothing better than stand-up comedy—

the lowest form of performance in his eyes. Then Williams played an old man in an obscure production of a Tennessee Williams play and silenced his critics with his complete and utter immersion into the character.

He began to impress his teachers one by one. In particular, he was adept at creating characters out of thin air. When he wasn't doing that, he was pulling off intimate, exact impressions of public figures that offered up just the right amount of satire. Williams was good at his characters because he was great at impressions. But the inspiration for memorable characters (like the ones we all got to know during his television and film career) only comes to those with a refined imagination.

His years as a loner in a mansion fit for10 more families began to manifest themselves in the freewheeling stream-of-consciousness improvisational skills that he was developing. Not only were his characters entertaining but they were pulled from thin air at his whim. By the end of his tenure at Juilliard, he had become a master of improv and comedy. Almost in direct opposition to the wishes of his teachers, who were still able to instill in him a love of drama, Williams became a comedian—if not in name.

Many were surprised at his breakout performance in *Good Will Hunting* many years after this. He seemed to be just as capable at producing solemn emotions in his audience as he was at eliciting laughs. Where could this have come from? It's quite simple.

He spent his young adult years at Juilliard. He had it within him the entire time, but his comedy made the world blind to it. Gone were the days where a performer was expected to be a "triple-threat" as they might say. Williams seemed to be the exception to that new rule.

So, when it came to pass that Williams developed all of these skills and reached the pinnacle of his education—they cut him loose. An instructor literally told him that they had nothing else they could teach him. Before he received his degree, he left Juilliard and began pursuing his own dreams. Later, Williams would return to the school to receive an honorary doctorate, long after reaching the heights of his career. Williams remained ever grateful for his time there.

He started a scholarship that gave a full ride to a promising young actor and maintained it to his death. He was the man responsible for sending a young Jessica Chastain to Juilliard, rocketing her to stardom. His influence was felt there for many years before and after his passing.

After leaving Juilliard, it was not a time for passing, but rather a time for new beginnings. Williams met his first wife and they moved back to San Francisco to start a life together. Williams was a man, wed and happy, and starting his journey to stardom. Where that journey started, however, did not seem so obvious as it does now.

Around this same time, stand-up comedy became popular in a way that it had never been before. People like Jerry Seinfeld, Steve

Martin, and Richard Pryor were turning into huge stars. Williams was likely inspired by this movement and decided to try it out for himself. That would begin the next portion of his life and the beginning of his legacy. From this moment on, his brand of humor came shining through; it was vulgar but always intelligent. If you are unfamiliar with the subject material, you have been warned — he pulls no punches.

Making it in Stand-Up

Robin Williams during one of his first televised performances:

"[After a minute of silence from the crowd] …I have gone too far into the land of strangeness. But, since I've kind of lost you, come into my mind and see what it's like when a comedian eats the big one…"

For every new comedian, there is a number you must know: five. Five minutes is all you have to entertain your audience. It is all the time given to you for your first sets, usually at an open-mic in a second-rate comedy club or bar. You must go from unlikable nobody to the (hopefully) drunken audience's best friend and confidante in the time it takes to use the restroom. It is no easy task and those that are proficient at it seem to wield some sort of magic that seems foreign to all but the most observant of fans. It can be a nerve-wracking experience, but it also carries with it a great sense of pride and accomplishment. There's just nothing quite like it.

Williams seemed to channel the base instincts of the profession. He seemed every bit the sharp city-dwelling comic, but he performed with the energy and loquaciousness of a medieval court jester. Truly, to those that discovered him early on, he seemed like a comedic prophet — built from something that others had no part in.

For Williams, it must have always seemed like a good fit. It was a perfect outlet for his ridiculous and occasionally uncomfortable character acting. Plus, he could take life exactly as seriously as he pleased. So, when he got to San Francisco with his new wife, his primary goal was to become a comedian. First, he had to pay the rent.

Williams began working odd jobs, usually in the service industry, sometimes at restaurants. He did this until he could find a way to get himself noticed. That moment came to him in the form of an audition for a comedy club — in the standard open-mic 5-minute format. Some might struggle to get their feet underneath them in a new situation like this, not Williams.

He began his comedy career not doing comedy at all. He worked for a bar/comedy club called the "Holy City Zoo" as a bartender until they gave him a chance to perform. Once he did, it was off to the races.

His first set was a satirical take on Franz Kafka's *Metamorphosis* — though that was the only thing high-brow about the bit. In *Metamorphosis*, the narrator is a failed business man that awakes in his room to find himself transformed into a hideous insect-like creature. The rest of the novel is a modernist reflection on the nature of existence. Though the novel is weird, it is not inherently funny.

Williams turned the premise into a surreal joke about masturbation. He was the narrator, but instead of turning into a bug, his character cannot leave his room because he can't stop masturbating. Eventually his penis grows in size, filling the room and preventing his escape. It's a great indicator of the things to come in Williams' career. Always funny, he would sometimes veer into the existential—perhaps that is what made his presence so unique.

At any rate, his performance was a hit in the comedy club. The 50 or so people in the audience were in stitches and Williams had the nod he needed to continue and look for more opportunities. His light seemed to be growing by the minute.

He was being heavily influenced by a comedian by the name of Jonathan Winters throughout this time and his entire life previous. Williams would list Winters as his biggest influence and it was never particularly close. Winters was an old holdout from a different era who had a career that lasted through six decades of American culture.

His comedy was a mainstay in Williams' life, along with other important comedians from that era. Winters was a favorite of the original host of *The Tonight Show*, Jack Paar, and got his big break in that arena. Nearly 40 years later, Winters would receive a lifetime achievement from Robin Williams, himself. There was nothing so important to the rise of Robin Williams than the comedy of Jonathan Winters.

Williams began to create his own brand of comedy and work in new bits that he thought of. Some of his early work is very interesting, aside from the Kafka-esque nod to masturbation. Williams liked to work different characters into his set, often coming onto stage as one person and then leaving the stage as another. It was rare that you saw his real self at any point. But he knew when to let you in — like in the joke at the beginning of the chapter.

His Shakespeare joke is what led to that breakdown and subsequent riffing at the opening of the chapter. He would, usually as a character with a heavy accent, disappear from the stage and enter again as a Shakespearean figure, speaking in Elizabethan. Almost always, the joke would begin:

"I would like to do Shakespeare's only unknown piece, 'That's the Way I Lick It' ... It's a bleak night my Lord. Look! The moon like a testicle hangs low in the sky. This bodes not well. ... Anon, post-haste, let's get a larger crowd in here. Free Cocaine! There's no luck. Does anyone have drugs to ease my pain? My Kingdom for a Quaalude! … It is the end! I must go, for I cannot come here, and yet, it has been brief, 'tis over, and the lights do turn bright."

The joke failed in this instance because he went into a strange tirade as a character— losing himself and the audience in the process.

One of his most famous recordings from this time was titled, "Reality: What a concept." It was his first comedy album and included a great deal of material from his beginning period. One of the best portions is an interpretation of William F. Buckley discussing *Goldilocks and the Three Bears:*

"First of all, let's examine her name, 'Goldi' the Aryan stereotype combined with 'lox' the Jewish soul food. Obviously, that combines to create a sort of bourgeoisie archetype. She is in confrontation with, of course three bears. They are not brown bears, they are not dark bears, they're 'third-world' bears. In this case, I am using Goldilocks as an example of Imperialism expanding outwards. Towards the minor race, countries, the third-world countries of the three bears…"

The best part about this joke is the accuracy of the academic sentiment. Williams, a purchaser of a great amount of schooling, would be very familiar with the academic zest for turning seemingly inconsequential coincidence into world-burning revelation. It was also a great showcase for his ability to play almost any character — having switched to Buckley directly out of another less-than-motherly figure that had been driven to drink by her children.

Drugs were a constant topic in many of Williams' comedy bits. After all, he practically grew up amid the biggest drug movement in history. Eventually that would come to play a large part in his personal life. He would overuse substances to the point that it impacted his personal relationships. For the time being, however, drugs were still funny to him and he took his best shots.

A famous joke of his begins:

"I haven't taken acid since I was 16. I went to my high school prom on acid, saying, 'No, Mr. Smith, I'll have Becky back in this dimension real soon! Wings! We've got to get those snakes coming out of your eyes fixed!'

Another dealt with cocaine:

"…It's a nice thing though, cocaine. Mmm, what a wonderful drug. Anything that makes you paranoid and impotent, get me more of that. Oh, what a strange thing to do. There's also something called freebasing. It's not free, it costs more than your house, it should be called 'home basing.'"

"Here's a little warning sign that you have a cocaine problem: First of all, if you come home to your house, you have no furniture, and your cat's going. 'I'm out of here, prick.' Warning one."

"Number two. If you have this dream that you're doing cocaine in your sleep and you can't fall asleep and you're doing cocaine in your sleep and you can't fall asleep and you wake up and you're doing cocaine — bingo."

"Number three. If on your tax form it says $50,000 for snacks: Mayday. You've got yourself a cocaine problem."

This would be something that would follow Williams around until the time of his death. But it had yet to begin to affect him. Instead he was headed straight forward in his career and decided that it was time to move to the best place in the world to make it: Los Angeles.

His time in San Francisco was at an end but he left the city in a better way than he found it by creating what critic Gerald Nachman called the "comedy renaissance" for the city. But there was a limit to what it could do for his career and he had to make the decision to leave to become the person that we remember and love.

There, in L.A., he would find mild success as a television character actor and started to build a reputation. He would perform for the revamped *Laugh-in* due to a chance encounter with a Hollywood producer named George Schlatter. Schlatter produced quite a few comedy shows over the years and recognized a talent when he saw one.

He was trying to revive his biggest hit: *Rowan & Martin's Laugh-in.* It was a variety show that brought in guest comics to do sketches and famously feature Richard Nixon in one of its episodes. He needed new comics and gave this up-and-comer the chance he was waiting for. Schlatter knew that, eventually, he would be on the right side of an important figure in show business.

Starting in 1977, at the age of 26, Williams would make his debut on the screen for a national audience. His renown began to grow, at least locally, and he was given a chance to do an HBO stand-up special. In this current age, an HBO special is a litmus test for who has really made it. Williams helped make that a reality with his performance. The *Laugh-in* revival did not do well but Williams was unaffected. Many times, a cancelled show can spell doom for a young actor's career, but Williams was still full-speed ahead.

Reality: What a Concept

As Williams went on with his career, the effects of performing stand-up began to wear on him. Many have complained about the "always-on" type of personality they are required to have when performing on a daily basis. Williams took that to another level. Maintaining his energy level was a constant drain on his psyche. As his mental defenses began to fail, he started to fill in the gaps with drugs and alcohol.

Williams would say later:

"It's a brutal field, man. They burn out. It takes its toll. Plus, the lifestyle—partying, drinking, drugs. If you're on the road, it's even more brutal. You gotta come back down to mellow your ass out, and then performing takes you back up. They flame out because it comes and goes. Suddenly they're hot, and then somebody else is hot. Sometimes they get very bitter. Sometimes they just give up. Sometimes they have a revival thing and they come back again. Sometimes they snap. The pressure kicks in. You become obsessed and then you lose that focus that you need."

As he began to film his greatest stand-up special yet, it became clear that he was developing substance abuse issues. He professed to cocaine use during this time, though he said he never used while he was onstage. But, it seemed like every other show began to wilt under the haze of the previous night's hangover. Critics began to question the longevity of his comedy style. It seemed as if he got more frenetic the longer he performed to the point one critic wondered if his mind could "reverse into a complete meltdown".

His style always seemed to be right on the edge of insanity. He would transfer in and out of different characters so fast that the audience sometimes had trouble keeping up. It was always worth it if you could, so he was never hurt by it. But, to the close observer, it appeared that—if ever he was tripped up—that he would fly off the tracks immediately. It's almost as if his mind was on edge and could not be contained. If it ever was fully unleashed, it would be a danger to himself and those around him.

In a way, that's exactly what happened as his cocaine use turned into abuse. The abuse was driven by his near-constant fear that he would lose the spark that he was given. He stated in an interview for Playboy, "There's that fear—if I felt like I was becoming not just dull but a rock, that I still couldn't speak, fire off or talk about things, if I'd start to worry or got too afraid to say something ... If I stop trying, I get afraid."

Luckily for him, this never spilled over to his professional side and he was on the cusp of his first great accomplishment as an entertainer. As his television career was taking off, he took the opportunity to record a couple shows and put that together into a comedy album.

The album would eventually be called *Reality: What a Concept*. It was an instant hit, careening through the Billboard Comedy charts to number 10 and stayed there for some time. Williams would be getting most of his press from his television appearances, but the comedy album established him in the annals of comedy's greatest talents. This is one of the reasons Billy Crystal would later remember him as "one of comedy's brightest stars".

There are any great moments in this album, as it represents a raw and untouched version of Williams before his fame had really set in and began to affect his material. All the bits from this album came directly from his tortured and hilarious mind. Like this next joke in which he impersonates a deranged, funhouse mirror version of Fred Rogers from *Mister Rogers' Neighborhood:*

"It's a beautiful day in the neighborhood... oh, damn, someone stole my sneakers. Let's do some wonderful things today, boys and girls; but first, do you mind if I take some more medication? It helps the day go a little bit slower. There we go. Now we're gonna do some wonderful experiments you can do around the house. Let's put Mr. Hamster in the microwave, okay?... He knows where he's going. BEEP! Pop goes the weasel! That's severe radiation. Can you say, "severe radiation"? Oh, look, you got a little balloon now."

It wouldn't be much of a stretch to say that Williams didn't take much time to classify himself out of the "family" comedy milieu. His jokes were colorful and absurd, but they never failed to show a mirror to reality. Quite frankly, there were some places in America that were not (and never had been) like the familiar Mister Rogers' neighborhood. Although he wasn't specifically making that point, his comedy was always insightful enough to get your mind into a different place.

However, although Williams was not the type to write and perform jokes that catered to middle Americans and families, his first big break would be a family show that almost everyone from that era would remember as good old-fashioned entertainment. He would walk on to a Hollywood set and blend right in immediately—but he had to do it as the consummate outsider. It was right up his alley.

Mork and Mindy

If you are old enough to remember watching Mork and Mindy, then you might also be old enough to remember where it all started. But, that's putting the cart before the horse. There were several different dominoes that needed to fall before Williams would get his opportunity to showcase his talents to the world. It starts with a classic television show and the capriciousness of a child.

When the producer of the hit television show *Happy Days* needed an idea, he didn't hesitate to reach as deep into his bag of tricks as he needed to. We all have heard of the term "jumping the shark" as it has leaked from Hollywood into the popular lexicon. It's a term that means to sell out or to completely give up on the idea of your show to get "butts in seats". That term was invented to describe the later stage of *Happy Days.*

It wasn't a termed coined out of wordplay or coincidence either. They literally had Henry Winkler jump over a shark while on water skis during an episode in their fifth season. If you watch the episode, it is a complete mystery how television like this was palatable to viewers in that era of entertainment. The schmaltzy music, alone, is enough to get any modern day 12-year-old to turn the channel immediately.

In our era of fake reality, realism (however constructed or contrived) is given top billing. We want gritty situations with hard answers, even in our comedy. That must be why it is so shocking to see a too-old Henry Winkler skiing behind a boat driven by a twenty-something Ron Howard. All of that might have been acceptable if The Fonz wasn't still wearing his signature leather jacket over some tight 1970s beach shorts. But, that's how it went back then.

So, suffice to say that *Happy Days* had no qualms about doing episodes that deviated widely from its established structure. So, naturally, when Garry Marshall — the previously referred-to executive — needed advice on where to take the show next, he asked his 7-year-old son. Apart from being the show's apparent demographic, Marshall went to that well because he knew that television was evolving and, like with Sinatra in the 40's and the Beatles in the 60's, the old guys that were on top had to look to new talent to stay there.

He recalled for an interview in *New York* magazine, celebrating the release of a hit Williams movie in the 90s: "My 7-year-old son Scott was reluctant to watch *Laverne & Shirley* or *Happy Days* or any show I did. So, I asked him, 'What *do* you like?' He said, 'I only like space.' I told him, 'I don't do space.' He said, 'Well you *could* do it.' So, I asked him, 'How would *you* do space in *Happy Days?*' And he said, 'It could be a dream.'

That's all that it takes to create a star sometimes. The writers for the show were looking for a great foil to Fonzie — the show's breakout star and a transient who lives in Ron Howard's house in the show. The thing is, Fonzie was already over the top. He was a 1970s actor doing an exaggerated 1950s greaser impression for an audience that, again, had mostly been unborn in the 1950s.

It still worked great, being a comedy show, but the premise needed a constant influx of new ideas to keep it fresh. Enter Robin Williams.

Williams got the nod to audition for the role by the grace of being in an acting class with Marshall's sister. They brought him in, garbed in colorful suspenders, and asked him to make the character really "alien". They asked him to show them how he though an alien would sit in a chair. So, Williams walked up to a couch like he had never seen it before in his life and flung himself upside down so that he was sitting on his head. He smiled wide, like he had completed a tough task excellently. They had found their alien.

It's almost a cliché to think that someone so "out there" as Robin Williams would get their start playing an alien on a throwback show about the 1950s. It just reads like one of his off-the-wall jokes that he would tell an audience of hysterically confused comedy fans. But, he was an instant fit in the role to the surprise of nobody that knew him.

Winkler would proclaim, "My job stopped being about remembering lines or moves, but to keep from laughing. And yet, Robin was so shy it was hard for him to speak. He did ask me, 'After a day of this, how do you perform at the Comedy Store?' I told him, 'After this, you really don't have the energy to perform at night.'"

Williams would not stop performing as a stand-up comedian for many, many years.

But his primary focus became acting in television. That part was not even entirely up to him. He had to because of his immense and sudden popularity. As it turned out. Marshall doubled down on his son's initial idea. He decided that the episode with Mork would not be a simple one-off that they could write out of whatever *Happy Days* canon existed. Instead, it would be a real event and it would happen in a separate city — though confusingly in the same timeline it could be assumed.

Williams was in a great position as Mork for the short time that it was on the air. He was given the ability to improvise most of his lines — the writers knowing that would be equal to or greater than whatever they could come up with. And, when Williams was asked to star in the new production they were calling *Mork and Mindy*, he was a household name almost immediately.

By the end of the show's first season, it would regularly bring in 60 million viewers. Take this number with a grain of salt, however, as the ratings for television have fallen progressively for the past couple of decades — especially for sitcoms. It was still a huge success in his time, however, and the press was all over it.

By the next Spring, Williams appeared on the cover of *Time* magazine and was the star to watch for anyone that knew anything. For one, his stardom was especially lucrative, considering he had such a huge sway with children. This would be a common thread throughout his whole career. Despite the vulgarity and lewdness of his actual stand-up comedy, children would be drawn to him for decades to come. Williams was a child-at-heart in a very genuine way and the children that saw him knew immediately that they had a friend in him.

They began to plaster his face on anything they could get ahold of. They put his face on lunchboxes, posters, cards, toys, coloring books — if a kid bought it, they could get a Mork version. The audience for *Happy Days* was so large that a single episode could create a spin-off.

The episode in which Mork appears is quite interesting, in and of itself. It was originally written, as stated, to be a dream. Even then, the writers wanted to be sure that they didn't write themselves into a hole — especially not one that would change their entire canonical world so quickly. But, considering the success of *My Favorite Martian* in the decade before, they felt they had enough of a license to do so.

The episode is centered around Mork's attempt to kidnap Richie Cunningham and bring him back to his alien superiors (henceforth named as the "Orkans") for further study on human anatomy. The Fonz must stop this plan and save his friend. Mork, in one of the better jokes of the episode, proclaims his superiority because he is from the "future" …the 1970s. At the end, everything gets tied up in a little bow like in most sitcoms and the characters are shown sleeping soundly and dreaming.

When Marshall and the other executives decided that they were going to create a spinoff for the show, they realized they couldn't leave that episode as a dream. It might compromise the writing of the future *Mork and Mindy* staff. So, they re-edited the ending scene to show Mork erasing the memories of his passing in their minds and returning to the "future" to live anew.

As Mork in the titular role for his television show, Williams would improvise the habits and dialect of his shrill, nasally character to great effect. His primary focus is to "study" humans but it is revealed in the opening episode that this is just a ploy for the other Orkans to get rid of Mork because humor isn't permitted on their planet. Mork, it can be assumed, didn't fit in there either. But, as he trots around the pilot in a suit that he put on backwards, it became clear to everyone involved that Robin Williams belonged on the screens of American entertainment.

Personal Life and Struggles

As most find out eventually, stardom doesn't always lead to a charmed life. There are many who cannot handle the pressure and leave before they ever become anything for that very reason. The rest must learn how to cope with an existence that is beyond bizarre and live as an image that is considered precious or infamous by most people they meet.

Williams' struggles were made from the same cloth and he regularly used substances and dangerous living to cope with his newfound purpose and position. It wasn't at all uncommon for comedians and musicians to overindulge to the point of danger in those times — as it is not uncommon now. However, society still turned a bit of a blind eye to these things. There was not the same push to enter rehabilitation programs as there is today. Instead, it was seen as a part of that person and not a problem that is able to be solved entirely.

For instance, Williams credits comedian Richard Pryor for giving him the license to go on stage and talk about the issues that were important in his life. Through this, he was able to find some kind of way to cope with the anxieties and insecurities that haunted him when he was not performing. Pryor was a famously prolific substance abuser himself, having doused himself in alcohol and lit himself on fire during a cocaine-fueled psychosis. He would later wave a lit match at one of his shows and remark, "What's that? Richard Pryor running down the street."

Williams greatly admired this approach to comedy and wished to emulate it as much as he could. In a way, that was likely a partial cause of his substance-abusing behavior. To tell those stories, you must live it. However, there is always a price to pay and it never seems like the exchange is equal.

For Williams, his use of cocaine was gradually turning into an addiction and it began to affect his personal life. Williams was a new father and the difference between his desire to raise a family and dependence on addictive substances was creating a rift in his personality. Many would claim that Williams just had a way about him in which he was "always on". In a way, that's what got him his biggest role as Mork. In another way, it is a kind of prison to be expected to be "on" all the time.

That's why the death of John Belushi was so impactful on Williams. Williams and Belushi were friends in the business and regularly partied together and would go on infamous binges. Belushi suffered from the same disease, an incredibly funny man himself, he found himself enveloped in drugs and finally passed away due to an overdose on what is known as a "speedball".

Speedballs are especially dangerous and were the drug of the era for people in the 1970s and 1980s. It essentially consists of both cocaine and heroin—combining two of the most powerful drugs in one experience. The effects were disastrous. The danger of both of those substances lies primarily in the cardio-vascular system and this drug gives the heart two different signals at the same time. It can be described as great euphoria followed by tremendous depression. The heroin-soaked mind can be conscious and awake in a way that would be impossible with the drug alone. It is a deadly thing and it killed John Belushi and many others.

Williams, as it turned out, was with Belushi very near to his death and was part of the binge that lead to it. He was subpoenaed by a grand jury and asked for his testimony during the proceedings. It struck him in a way that he had been able to avoid so far, as a member of the social elite. Belushi was a great friend of his and the party suddenly turned into a funeral procession. All of Hollywood shook afterwards, but it was particularly difficult for a young Robin Williams.

Williams would say in an interview for New York magazine, People would come up and say, 'Are you a friend of Bill W.?' I'd think, Did I do drugs with Bill W.? Did I sleep with him? But, I didn't have to join a group. Zach was about to born, and I didn't want to miss it because I was coked up or drinking. I was hideous enough felling hung over without a baby screaming. I mean, there are times when you think, God made babies cute so you don't eat them—imagine if you're loaded."

Following the loss of his friend, Williams began to focus his efforts on exercise—cycling, in fact. The owner of the bicycle shop Williams would frequent at that time claimed that Williams believed that cycling had saved his life. It makes sense, being able to push yourself towards a productive goal has long been a capable panacea for those hoping to avoid the terrors of addiction and depression.

Williams was unable to maintain complete sobriety for the rest of his life and it was, as is typical, a story of tragedies and victories. However, one fact can be gleaned, he never did cocaine again after the death of Belushi, stating, "No. Cocaine – paranoid and impotent, what fun. There was no bit of me thinking, ooh, let's go back to that. Useless conversations until midnight, waking up at dawn feeling like a vampire on a day pass. No."

He would struggle with alcoholism for the rest of his life, checking himself into treatment centers more than once. But it was not a life spent entirely wasted. His family life was filled with genuine love and the regular orderly track of life. His first wife gave him his son Zachary Williams and Robin spent a great deal of his time trying to be a good father for him. However, his marriage to his mother was limited in its breadth and doomed to eventual failure.

During the time following Zachary's birth, the couple had a smattering of nannies and caretakers that would assist them in raising the child, considering their hectic lives. Of those, there was Marsha Garces, a lover of fabric and textiles, that lived at their ranch in the Napa Valley area of California. The child had trouble with his previous nannies and was prone to throwing tantrums.

His time with Garces seemed to stop that right in its tracks. Zachary cut back on the tantrums and his relationship with her blossomed overnight. When Williams needed an assistant for his next tour, he had her in mind, thanks to her stellar performance as a nanny. Right about this time, Robin's wife left to go live with a boyfriend somewhere else and the door was open for a romance to blossom.

However, it did not occur quickly or naturally. Williams was far too caught up in himself to attract an intelligent girl like Marsha. There was no romance to be found for here when he was about as broken as a man could become without losing it entirely.

Marsha had a similar effect on Robin that she did on Zachary. During that time, he began to believe that he was worthless and a bad person. Marsha was there to constantly tell him that the only bad thing about himself was how he perceived himself to be. If he wasn't so messed up, he wouldn't be so messed up. He began to believe that he could be loved by someone worthwhile that truly believed in him.

His relationship with her eventually wilted, as well. This came as a surprise to many that saw them as a power couple in Hollywood. Marsha was involved in every aspect of his life and frequently served as a go-between for Robin and the many responsibilities being a big star entailed. However, by 2008, the couple filed for divorce and parted forever.

Williams would marry again a few years before his death and by all accounts the marriage was happy while it lasted. More than anything, however, Williams considered his children to be his legacy and found himself constantly surprised by their talents and the depths of which he cared about them.

Film Career

The next stage in Williams' career and the primary method for which he became famous is his extensive and lauded filmography that will go down as one of the most accomplished as far as comedians go. Williams was getting plenty of interest as a film actor, but many of the roles did nothing to advance his career. However, he was able to hone his on-screen skills through the experience he got from *Mork and Mindy* and these minor roles.

Throughout his career, he could find help by working with fantastic actors that helped deepen his already excellent understanding of the craft. For example, while filming a movie called *Insomnia* he met and learned from acclaimed actor Robert De Niro. He learned how to sulk and seethe behind the eyes from the man who perfected it in *Taxi Driver*.

He was good friends with Billy Crystal, an acclaimed actor in his own right, that had a great deal of experience in romantic comedies and, in general, acting on screen. His work with *When Harry Met Sally* is a great example of a comedian showing dramatic acting chops and showed how Crystal could go toe-to-toe with Williams.

Woody Allen, some years later, would cast them together in his surreal comedy *Deconstructing Harry*. There was something about their relationship that just seemed to work. Right around that time, they also appeared in an episode of *Friends* together, at the height of the show's popularity.

Regardless of his influences, he would find a way to create his own legacy through the work he did in films geared entirely towards him. The first and, perhaps, most important leading role he took was in *Good Morning Vietnam.* He took it just after his role in *Mork and Mindy* ended, and it was clear he was desperate to show he was more than just a lead in a schmaltzy television sitcom.

The 1988 film was about a disc jockey who worked for the military in the middle of the Vietnam war. He was supposed to just give out the news and the weather and get off air, but instead spent a good deal of this time acting irreverent and ridiculous for the entertainment of his fellow soldiers.

The film is remarkable for many reasons. It was a critical and commercial success, but it was almost entirely driven by the performance of Williams. Roger Ebert had this to say about the film:

"What is inspired about "Good Morning, Vietnam," which contains far and away the best work Williams has ever done in a movie, is that his own tactics are turned against him. The director, Barry Levinson, has created a character who is a stand-up comic - he's a fast-talking disc jockey on Armed Forces Radio during the Vietnam War, directing a nonstop monologue at the microphone. Everything in his world is reduced to material for his program... Levinson [the director] used [the script] as a starting point for a lot of Williams' monologues, and then let the comedian improvise. Then he put together the best parts of many different takes to create sequences that are undeniably dazzling and funny. Williams is a virtuoso.

You read that correctly, in a Hollywood movie in which the subject material is the Vietnam war, they allowed Williams to essentially create a stand-up set as a character in the world they were creating. It was a perfect situation for him and it allowed his talents to be placed within a context that really set him apart from other actors who might have been in that role.

The next film he did of note was released the very next year in 1989. It was called *The Dead Poet's Society* and had a much different overall tone. The concept was the same for his casting, however. The film required someone who was familiar, yet who the audience would believe did not actually trust in the overall establishment — commiserating with the youthful boy's school protagonists.

What was really notable about his memorable performance was how easily he could turn into a soft-spoken English teacher that had more to him than met the eye. He could recite Byron and Whitman in a way that seemed as if he really believed they knew the words that could save your life. It was a tour de force of comedic acting. Really, it was just enough of a comedy to keep you interested. The meat of the movie lies in the loyalty that Williams inspires in his students. It went on to inspire people generations younger than him and is one of the roles that most contributed to his legacy as a film actor.

His next role paired him with legendary actor Jeff Bridges, right in the middle of his heyday in the early 90s. In a strange turn, Bridges is actually working as a radio jockey and has a strange run-in with a homeless man whose life he affected. This film is carried by Williams' pathos and strangeness, but it really works as an allegory for William's earlier life.

The disk jockey is a "shock jock" that became popular during that time on radio. During one of his insane monologues, something he says inspires a madman to commit a mass shooting at a restaurant in Manhattan. He becomes suicidal and drunk and ruins his career—ending up working in a video store with a girlfriend. He tries to kill himself but is mistaken for a homeless person and attacked on the street by a gang.

Williams' character saves him and is able to show him perspective. Without ruining the twist, there is something in their past that connects them, and they are both able to find their own way. (As an aside, this is a film directed by a member of Monty Python and Williams' character is maddeningly obsessed with finding the Holy Grail as in the Monty Python movies.)

With these roles on his resume, Williams could be cast in basically anything he wanted to work in. His life firmly in the bounds of his family and children at this point, his next task was to be cast in an animated film. This film would be the Disney movie *Aladdin*. Williams was initially hesitant, not wanting to contribute to the Disney machine. But he agreed to act in it if he was not sold as a toy or branded as such. Disney agreed but later recanted in a very big way.

Still, the movie was a smash hit and opened the door for other famous actors to contribute to animated movies as a genuine career choice. He was even nominated for a Grammy for an original song that he sang as the Genie character. For kids all over the country, the Genie was their new hero and he likely worked his way directly into the hearts of his own children.

However, the best, most impactful role he ever played was that of a therapist in the Matt Damon/Ben Affleck debut film *Good Will Hunting*. Williams plays the role of a therapist to a talented, but broken day laborer that has latent high-level mathematics abilities. It is a heart-wrenching story of absolution and ambition that Williams plays with the incisiveness of any of the great "dramatic" actors. There is nothing left on the page that Williams doesn't take full advantage of.

The brilliance of the film is that it doesn't set any expectations for its characters. Williams, a therapist, is perhaps the most forlorn of all the characters — losing the love of his life to cancer. He still tries to help people, even though he can barely go on himself. Damon, a nobody, contains the talent of a NASA scientist, but there is no one around to care.

The film was created on a budget of only $10 million but grossed over $225 million worldwide. It was a smash-hit and ever more proof that Williams was capable of turning any script into gold and any character into a real, living person.

Death and Legacy

"He made us laugh. Hard. Every time you saw him. On television, movies, nightclubs, arenas,

hospitals, homeless shelters, for our troops overseas and even in a dying girl's living room for her last wish. He made us laugh, big time.

I spent many happy hours with Robin on stage. The brilliance was astounding, the relentless energy was kind of thrilling. I used to think that if I could just put a saddle on him and stay on for eight seconds I was going to do ok."

--Billy Crystal at the 66th Emmy Awards Show in honor of Robin Williams

Williams' career would go on for a steady click for some time after. In fact, some of the movies that aren't mentioned here have had a huge impact on lives that would another book to completely examine. Eventually his fame reached an apex and he took to the somber duty of churning out family comedies for the sake of his children and his career. He would never reach the excellence of *Good Will Hunting* but he found several meaningful roles regardless.

Towards the end of his life, it seemed that Williams was finally ready to come back into the lives of Americans after an extended hiatus from the limelight. He was filming a *Night at the Museum* sequel and it is unlikely a return to the big screen would catch anything but great admiration from the public. However, life had other plans for Robin.

Starting in 2013, Williams began to experience a tremor in his hand that would persist longer than was natural. Slowly but surely, his mental condition deteriorated to the point that he was living in constant stress and fear. Throughout his whole life he had been badgered by these forces that seemed to be in his head. Now, there were real chemical reasons for him to feel this way.

He would say often, "I just want to reboot my brain." According to his later autopsy, he had a rare form of dementia that gets progressively worse over time. He was diagnosed with Parkinson's, incorrectly, and withheld the information of his sickness for some time. Doctors who were privy to his medical information would call it one of the "worst pathologies" they had ever seen.

On August 11, 2014 Williams hung himself with his belt at his home in California. There were no signs of drugs or alcohol, simply the strange bodies called Lewy bodies that indicate his form of dementia. His wife describes the time before his suicide as a "spike in paranoia" and it's likely the disease was too hard on him—resulting in his decision to kill himself.

The world mourned, and it still does. His body was cremated and thrown into the San Francisco Bay, his home. There will never be another Robin Williams, though many will try. His effect and his presence were second-to-none. The world thought they had just stumbled onto the next great funny man. But what they really discovered was a friend, a father, a genius, and a kind soul. It will forever be a tragedy that a man, so loved by so many, would take his own life. The only thing we can do is continue to appreciate and understand his legacy in hopes that his time here on Earth made us better as people.

The only person that should be given top billing in Robin Williams story is Billy Crystal—his closest friend and brother-in-arms. This is the last part of the speech begun at the beginning of this chapter. But it does not have to be the last part of Robin Williams. Watch his work, remember his life and he will be alive for as long as we can remember:

"For almost 40 years he was the brightest star in a comedy galaxy. But while some of the brightest of our celestial bodies are actually extinct now, their energy long since cooled.

But miraculously, since because they float in the heavens so far away from us now, their beautiful light will continue to shine on us forever. And the glow will be so bright, it'll warm your heart, it'll make your eyes glisten and you'll think to yourselves, 'Robin Williams — what a concept.'"

Made in the USA
Middletown, DE
28 January 2022

59868284R00059